The Bottom Line

Profit Enhancement For the 21st Century

For

SMALL AND LARGE BUSINESS APPLICATION

WRITTEN BY

G.COLE HARNED

authorHOUSE™

1663 LIBERTY DRIVE, SUITE 200
BLOOMINGTON, INDIANA 47403
(800) 839-8640
WWW.AUTHORHOUSE.COM

First published by AuthorHouse 10/21/05

ISBN: 1-4208-5479-8 (sc)

Library of Congress Control Number: 2005905370

Printed in the United States of America
Bloomington, Indiana

This book is printed on acid-free paper.

DEDICATION

This book is dedicated to my wife, Pam, who with her support I was able to complete this work as well as get published. Her love and devotion to myself and our family has been unerring throughout our lives together.

This is also dedicated to all the business owners and management I am able to reach out to and help with this material. I well wish you all as you journey on the road to successful business enterprise!

GOOD LUCK
&
STAY FOCUSED
!!!

Letter from the Author;

Having spent most of my adult life in the food service business it has become very clear that without the proper knowledge your chances to fail are much greater than to succeed. The large corporations have the ability to hire people to handle the items I will talk about in this book. They hired me to perform these tasks. I have been very successful in this business and now I want to share much of what I have learned with you. I want to give to you the knowledge the big business owners have so you to can increase your chances to be successful in your business. Big or small this book will even the playing field and allow you to achieve results you never dreamed you could achieve.

You may be a new business owner, a frustrated business owner thinking it is time to get out, a potential buyer wanting to go into business, or perhaps you are working on climbing the ladder in one of the big corporations and want some added knowledge to help your career. When you complete this book you will know more than you ever knew in the past about opportunities to increase your value in either your own company or in someone else's company.

I will cover step by step each area that you must focus on to increase your potential to thrive in today's marketplace. There are no tricks to success; there are opportunities. What we will do as you read this book is review what opportunities you have for improvement and what to do about them. You will gain confidence that you can make a big difference in your future. In your own business it will mean thousands of dollars in increased profits. If buying a company I will show you where you can look at the information presented to you and identify where you can make changes to increase the profitability almost overnight. If you are just thinking of investing in a business this will give insight to what you must look for to thrive. Last but not least; if this is to help you improve your worth to a company, I will give you the tools to be comfortable in business meetings that you will be able to interact and understand opportunities that many of your co workers will have no idea about or how you know so much.

Before you begin I want to congratulate you on taking your first step to running a better business. My e-mail address is COLEHARNED@CS.

COM. If you have a one on one question that I can help with or if you want to send feedback to this book please feel free. I will do my best to respond to every piece of mail I receive.

Good Luck;

Cole Harned

PS- I have added blank note pages in each chapter. Make notes, make "to-do" lists, note down thoughts... this will help focus your direction as you act.

TABLE OF CONTENTS

IDENTIFY ISSUES

P&L STATEMENT 3
COGS 11
OTHER P&L ITEMS 25
UNSEEN ISSUES/ SETTING GOALS 29

CUTTING COST TO INCREASE PROFIT

FINDING QUICK CASH 37
ADDITIONAL SAVINGS: 43
COST OF GOODS AND INVENTORY 49
LABOR/OT 57
THEFT/WASTE 63
WASTE 69

LONG TERM SUCCESS

VENDOR RELATIONSHIP 75
BUILDING BUSINESS EQUITY 77
LISTEN 78
ADJUST AS NEEDED 80

GREAT SERVICE MEANS GREAT BUSINESS BUILDING SALES

VALUE OF GREAT SERVICE 87
POWER OF WORD OF MOUTH 89
VENDOR ADVERTISING HELP/LOW COST SOLUTIONS 92
POWER OF L.T.O.'S 97

REDUCING OVERHEAD

LANDLORD NEGOTIATIONS 105
UTILITIES 115
INSURANCE COMPANY.. 123
MISC: ALARMS, TRASH, EXTERMINATOR, LINENS/TOWELS/APRONS,
MUSIC, ETC.. 124

EXAMPLES OF COST SAVINGS TO PROFIT

FORM REVIEW PAGE.. 139

CONCLUSION

CONGRATULATIONS!!!! 147

IDENTIFY ISSUES

1 Profit and Loss Statement Importance

2 Cost Controls

3 Sales

4 Identify Issues Unseen/Setting Goals

P&L STATEMENT

Profit and loss statements are a major key to success. Everyone has heard this but in reality how many people really know how to read them? How to use them as a learning tool? A teaching tool? A tool that will not only cut costs but build sales and reduce employee turnover. Yes; you will accomplish all these if you use the Profit and Loss Statement to its fullest ability. As we go into this you may want to pull out your own P&L and make notes on it. You may find it needs more detail or perhaps you have made it so big it is of little use. Too much information is almost as bad as too little.

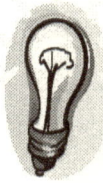

FACT: The more precise the document, the easier it is to understand, the more valuable the tool will become. A one-page document is all that is needed for most businesses. I have enclosed a P&L that I find complete and to the point as an example.

A P&L is like a visit to your family Doctor. A check up so to speak. It will tell you what went right, what went wrong, and most important where to look to improve your business. The one page document has some broad categories. All you want to do is narrow the hunt. See what the family Doctor has to say about your health. Once you have narrowed it down to an item or two then you can start into the detail viewing. This is going to the specialist. You would never go to a family Doctor for open-heart surgery, but he would direct you to a specialist who is better qualified to do surgery.

The key to a great P&L is that in just a few minutes you should be able to narrow down what is right and wrong and then be able to resolve the issue!

Labor

The specialist then takes over and may need additional information. Let's take something easy like cost of labor. This should include everyone who is on payroll plus all tax that is paid by either you or your employee. Additionally if there is a cost for someone to prepare the payroll such as a payroll check company these fees are usually a percent of the payroll and should also be included. This is everything that is in this category.

The following is a base payroll report:

NAME	SOCIAL SECURITY	WAGE/include tax/fee	HOURS WORKED	OVERTIME
A	123-45-6789	$9.55	40	3
B	987-65-4321	$8.50	38	0
C	222-22-2222	$8.50	28	0

The key here is keep it simple and direct. You will be able to track everything needed from this simple format. You must separate overtime since this is key to improving the bottom line. Also at the top of each payroll sheet always have the date which must include year. This will help later for tax preparation.

Note it has names, social security numbers or employee numbers, wage, salary or hourly, number of hours worked, overtime worked, and projected fees and taxes. The fees will vary slightly depending on which payroll service you may use. As we look down the report the first thing we make sure of is that the total is correct and has transferred over to the P&L right. The next thing to do is get a copy of the schedule and see if everyone worked the hours they were supposed to have worked. This is crucial because if every employee stayed just 15 minutes extra or came in just 15 minutes early it can really add up when the P&L comes in. The next item to review is overtime. Overtime is the number one reason for bad labor costs. The law states you must pay 1 and ½ times regular pay for any hours worked over 40 hours for all hourly employees. Some states even have laws that regulate if an employee works over an 8 hour shift this also must be considered overtime. Make sure you are well versed on your states laws regulating labor. The fines are steep for unfair employment practices.

The number one reason for high labor is overtime. You must pay 1 and ½ time regular hourly rate for all hours worked over 40 hours for all hourly employees!

Please note the information I have provided.

1 Labor Hours Worked
2 Schedule
3 Actual Labor Percent
4 Labor Percent with no Overtime
5 Labor Percent Following Schedule with no Overtime

Sales for this week in review $15,000

G. Cole Harned

Total Hours Paid For All Employees (Not Salary)	500 at $10 per hour avg.
Scheduled Hours	450 total
Actual Labor Percent	33.3%
Scheduled Labor Percent	30%
Over Used Labor For Week	$500
Overused Labor For Year On This Basis	$26,000

$26,000 overused from just slightly overusing your labor hours. One of the strongest tools you have for reducing labor is a good schedule!!!!!!!!! Spend as long as you need to perfect one then stick to it. The above example does not even include if there was any over time. The numbers could have been much worse. Imagine if the 50 extra hours was divided among 5 different employees. With that in mind you may only have 30 hours of overtime. Let's see what happens in that format...

Sales for the week in review	$15,000
Total Hours Paid Regular	470 at $10 per hour avg.
Overtime Paid	30 at $15 per hour avg.
Actual Labor Percent	34.3%
Overused Labor $	$675 week
Overused w/ Overtime for Year	$35,100

Over $35,000 that would be wasted. Every dime counts, every minute equals many dimes spent!!! Use the clock as your friend!!!

Note; we are taking for granted the schedule was made based on the business needs. I will do much more detailed review of using a schedule later in the book. At this point we are focusing on the P&L and identifying opportunities.

Now that we have identified what labor can do to help or hurt a business let's continue our review of the rest of the P&L.

The Profits are Taking Off.......
Hold on we have just begun!!!

NOTES

NOTES

COGS

The next category we come to is Cost of Goods. Otherwise known as COGS or Cost of Goods Sold. Again, this is a broad range of items but we are still at the family Doctor. You can separate this into two parts for ease review. All food items: any item used to make a product or the product itself to include beverages in one group we will call FOOD. The other group is PAPER. This includes everything used to prep the food, serve the food, or hold the food. Cups, lids, straws, napkins, plates, forks, knives, bags, sandwich wrap, etc. are in this group.

In this example the COGS group is at 40%. I projected that the total cost would be 32% so we have a problem. In the projection paper should have been 4% and food 28%. The paper in our P&L is 1% off running 5% while food is 7% high running 35%.

When both food and paper run high it is a strong indicator of theft or sales not being rung up! This shows complete product walking out the door. Indicates money probably changed hands and never made it to the register. On the other hand if just food is high it indicates a possible portioning issue, too high waste, or employees consuming product. If only paper is high, either the count of the inventory is wrong or there is high waste. For example: giving too many napkins, dropping items on the floors, or even employees using too many cups during a shift to get their own drinks while working.

This can include food being given to family and friends, or employees eating, and this not be taken into account. All food that is prepared and consumed even by employees should be accounted for. The food should be accounted for under discounted sales. This will give a true indication of COGS. This also encourages employees to not help themselves as much since they know it must be accounted for. You will reduce over portioning when you require accountability of all products for everyone.

Set a good example and always discount your own food also so the employees see this policy is for EVERYONE! The better you are at following the rules the better your employees will follow!

Other than theft as mentioned above there are only a few factors to high cost of goods. The biggest by far is waste/ over portion. Leftover products that cannot be sold needs to be tracked daily and even by shift.

A simple form, such as the one I have included, is an example of what to do.

PRODUCT	WASTE/SPOILED	LEFTOVER	COST LOST
ABC	5	3	$2.95
DEF	1	8	$5.90
HIJ	0	2	$4.65
TOTAL			*$13.50*

At the end of each shift see where you stand and then see what can be done to reduce this waste/ leftover problem. Could it be a specific shift or Manager causing most of the problems? This will guide you on a direction to solve the problem.

You must know where the product has gone. This will tell you who has a problem of over production. This will also help with your prep for the following week.

A note on prep: Even if you have prepped too much on a given day do not reduce the prep for the following day to overcome. Reduce your prep for the following week. What I mean is a Monday's business is more similar to the next Monday, a Tuesday to a Tuesday etc. If you cut back the following day then you can hurt your sales by running out of product. Plan ahead so you can act and not react!

After you have charted waste then work on reducing this to fewer than 3% of sales on a daily basis. Some days will be close to zero while others will be high. The overall number is the goal.

Keep in mind not to run out of product because this will hurt sales growth!

Portioning is the next concern. Any item that is hand portioned and can be pre portioned prior to serving should be done so. Meat, cheese, tuna salad, tomato slices, etc. can all be pre portioned to reduce over portion.

Have fun by holding contests for items to be portioned and see who can be the most consistently right! Have fun reducing cost and making more money! At the same time the employees will be happier and this will help reduce turnover!! Everyone wins in this situation. A happy work place also helps increase sales thereby increasing profits. One note to mention is sharing information with employees. If your employees know there is a problem or if they know what the goal you are trying to hit, it will be much easier to get them to buy into the program! Make sure as you see improvement you praise the work of all employees! Key to success!!!

The last thought on portion is going back to training. Everyone should know what the proper portion should be but also there is great benefit for new employees to have a chart near the workstation showing items and what the portion is so there is a constant reminder. Any home computer can be used to make a chart then go to an office copy place and have them laminate it so it can stay clean.

Small "cheat cards" to place in an employees pocket also helps. That way, when they are away from the chart, such as in a walk-in, in they can refer to their pocket card. Very low cost but very effective to reduce over portion.

We have reduced waste, improved our portioning, which will also improve quality, and now it is time to point the finger at our self.

Go ahead and take a second and point your finger at a door or wall near you. Turn your hand over and you will see that you have three pointed back at yourself. I heard this a long time ago and have tried to live my business life by the thought that every time I point a finger I am three times to blame. Did I train well? Did I push too hard? Were my expectations reasonable? Just something to keep in mind! Start shouldering the blame for failures and accept you can make a difference. When we blame others we walk through life believing everyone else is wrong and we are right. Bad thought process! We are all imperfect and we all accept blame for maximum results! A quick acronym I have used for years is T.E.A.M. or TOGETHER EVERYONE ACHIEVES MORE! No blame just team!

The next item that will help reduce cost of goods is completely in the control of the person placing our order for delivery. For this to work correctly you should have an idea of what your sales should be in the week upcoming, what product you will have on hand when the delivery arrives, an estimate of what waste will be, and an extra 10% to cover errors and business growth.

I like to have a very clean guide with no items on it that do not pertain to my business. Your vendor will only go so far to help you with this so you may need to spend a few minutes and make your own. After you get it complete you will have: **Product, product number, par level** (this is the amount you know you will need for the upcoming week for every item), a box for on hand, and a box for order. This one guide I will use for the entire month and when the month is done I will include it with my P&L, Labor Guides, Invoices, and Utility information in a file for the end of year tax prep. Each month will then have it's own guide, which will be easy to reference in the following year as you plan.

BASE SAMPLE ORDER GUIDE:

PRODUCT	PRODUCT CODE #	PRICE	ONHAND	PAR LEVEL	ORDER
A	123	.39	3	10	7
B	456	1.45	10	11	1
C	789	.78	2	2	0

As mentioned the guide should be specific to you. Once you get this set up then you can make copies and reuse over and over. Having a clean sheet is imperative to reduce cost of goods by reducing waste/spoilage, theft, over portion, over stocking. Par level, to recap, is what you must have for your business for the given order time frame. If you get an order a week then this is the number that will allow you to have enough product to make it until next delivery with a small extra for sales growth. When doing the order guide you must be aware of sales trends. If you have a consistent sales line week to week that's fine and use the same par for each week but if week three of each month is greater and week four is less then do a par level for each week. After doing your inventory, never at your desk but walking the store, then subtract what you have from your par and this is your order. Once set up this will not only save money but lots of time!

Key to ordering: Always walk the entire location and verify all on hand. Every storeroom, shelf, and closet must be reviewed to make an accurate order. Make notes......you will not remember everything! Plan to win by planning, plan to fail by not planning at all!

It will help to set up your store to make this easier. All food products grouped, all paper products grouped, and if possible have only one location for a product. There are some cases you have no choice, for instance if there are several drink stations, or you thaw frozen items in the cooler. On the most part you can significantly reduce inventory through organization. By reducing inventory you are keeping your money in the bank and not on the shelf, which will help cash flow. This will also greatly reduce theft. You say; "How could that be?" When you only order what you know you will need for a given time period and the time period is not up yet you run out of something only two things could have happened. The first is sales increased and that's great order extra, the other is somebody took something. A whole ham or turkey is easy to carry out with the trash.

To help reduce this possibility further; have all boxes broken down flat prior to leaving the door. This will help the dumpster but also remove the chance something is hidden inside the box!

There are many small items that can also help reduce COGS but we have covered the big hitters. You can see many opportunities once you start to really focus on the big picture. Like how many cups are employees wasting everyday? Buy plastic cups and put a name on them so everyone has their own cup. How many bags or boxes were dropped on the floor today? Are the employees giving a reasonable amount of napkins for an order or huge handfuls? Are the condiments handed out in handfuls with no regard to amount needed for the order? Are fountain drinks filled up properly with ice? This ensures greater quality but also reduces syrup usage. Have the soda fountains calibrated on a weekly basis. (The soda service company will generally do this free on a quarterly basis if asked.)

You will need a kit to set the soda machine mixture. The kit is called a Brix Kit. Your fountain drink distributor will provide this item. Get them to drop one by and while they are there have them teach you and your employees how to use the kit. Great savings for you in reduced syrup usage and improved product quality! This is great for both you and the soda company. Winning for both makes this an easy sell while increasing your profits!

I have left the easiest and probably the best cost of goods cutting method for last. This was on purpose. If you do not grasp all the items I have talked about and jump right to this one you will be leaving money on the table. Which somebody else picks up. Do everything we have talked about and you will significantly reduce costs. As you are implementing these ideas you need to set up meetings with your vendors. I need to explain the difference between a vendor and a distributor. A vendor or vendor representative is the person who represents a specific product or product line, i.e. soda or chicken would have two different vendors. The distributor is the person who brings you the goods. He is the person you contact to help you set up meetings with the vendors.

The vendor works to help you get the best cost available for each item. This is a person who could be on commission. Have a plan to look at additional product lines if they give you discounts on present items. In other words the same vendor you get mayo from also has mustard and ketchup. The vendor will lower the price for all three items if you give him the additional lines of business. This shows you want them to reduce your cost but you understand they are also reducing their pay. The vendor can offer new lines as they come out. A new product that is a fit for your business to help drive sales. Always keep the door open for your vendors.

Prior to the first vendor meeting spend a few minutes with the distributors representative and let them know why you wanted to meet with the vendors and what goal you have in mind. If you have no idea how low they will go then ask ballpark questions. " I am being charged _____ for mustard. I know that you have the account for the major burger chain in town and I was wondering what they pay?" The representative will explain that he is on a contract because of volume and it is different. Wrong!! The mustard is in his warehouse and should cost you the same if the product is not a brand specific item. You should not have to pay anymore than the big guy! Once you know this number, this is what you go after.

To recap what we are doing. We get the base price for each item at the same low cost as the big guy. Our delivery charge will be more but that has nothing to do with product cost. The products must be identical and not be branded by a competitor. The highest quality mustard, mayo, steak sauce are all items that are not bottled for specific companies. These are name brand products and you can get them at the reduced price. (A special sauce, a specific grade meat, or a logo packaged item you cannot get.) You cannot even compare the cost. You will have a better product quality at less price and GET YOU on an even playing field with the biggest companies you are competing with!!!!

You need to go through every single item on your order guide and see how many products are sitting in a warehouse at significantly lower cost that you can start buying. Most often it will even be a higher quality product! Be persistent with your distributor. Make sure they bring their warehouse price guide so you can talk specifics.

Some items you can get changed without even talking to the vendor! Get all these items off the list first. No need to waste time with a vendor when the distributor can take care of you. Make sure you list every item with the new agreed price and a date when this will take effect! If the date agreed upon arrives and the price is not reduced then you can demand a credit for the amount and continue to get credits until the price is corrected. Again; never leave money on the table. You will be about to buy top of the line product for less than you have been spending for the generic products you have been buying!

This will take time for you to review every item. Once the distributor knows what you want he can do most of the work before you even start meeting with any vendor. Many of the vendors will not even have to be met with because you will automatically get the best price. This will save time and money. We are having some fun now!

To repeat; keep track of every price for every product and make sure they bill you correctly. Always get a weekly order guide from your distributor to verify pricing!

Now that all the miscellaneous products are done, we will need to start meeting with vendors of specific items that you sell. These are meat products, cheese, soup, etc. These are the products that you need to first see about price decrease. After you get the best possible price then ask to have it locked in over 6 months to a year. This will make hitting a budget much easier. No surprises from a bad crop or meat prices skyrocketing. All dairy and meat should be locked in as well as items like coffee and ketchup. All these products fluxuate frequently. The more items you contract the more consistent your cost but also the easier it is for you to do follow up.

The last thing you will talk to your distributor about is his drop charge. This is the charge he adds to every product to bring them to you. There should be several categories. Dairy, Produce, Paper Goods, Frozen, and Dry Goods. Each will have a different percent of drop charge. The percent is different for various reason but there are two main ones: first the more volatile the product, the more ability to have loss for the distributor the higher the cost; and second is the distributor has an amount he must make at each stop to make a profit. He can never go under the number. Your negotiating power is somewhat limited for this matter.

It is paramount you have a good relationship with your distributor for them to want to help! Remember T.E.A.M: this applies for your distributor and vendors also! The better you do, the more you save, the greater chance you stay in business, the more money everyone makes long term.

This process is probably going to directly affect their income so you will have to be more creative to get help. First you must be prepared to offer something to them for reducing your cost. An example would be you get two deliveries a week. Each delivery is $1,200. You have the space to take only one delivery a week and increase the one delivery to $2,400. Offer this for a reduced drop percent. 100% of the time you will get this if you ask as I have said.

I know you need to make so much per stop. To decrease the drop cost I am willing to take only one delivery a week.

You will usually get a 1% drop off the total invoice. What you can then suggest is that you receive a drop size rebate. If the drop is over $2,000 you get ½ of a percent, over $2,500 get 3/4%, $3,000 and higher you get 1%. By offering it this way it shows you understand his or her business and are willing to help them also. The next item to discuss is a quick pay rebate. If you have the ability to pay every two weeks but have not because you do bills monthly ask about this rebate. "If I pay you twice a month instead of once you will carry less debt on your books from me? Will you give me ½% rebate for this?" Again, almost 100% of the time the answer will be yes. It costs him much more than ½% to carry that money. You will probably need to have a couple of meetings to accomplish the distributor work. There will need to be a contract agreement and the finance department as well as their legal department to draw this up. Do not give up and continue to call to get this complete. Two weeks is plenty of time to have this resolved.

 You have just saved from 2% to 5% off your total food bill by just being smart to needs. If your cost of goods is $5000 per week for 52 weeks or $260,000 per year you just put $5,200 to $13,000 in your pocket! If your thought this process was a pain just remember what you accomplished as you deposit this into your account!!! Get this in writing and request checks sent to you quarterly for drop size rebates. You do not want them to deduct this amount from upcoming invoices; it is too easy to lose track of the amount and you never see the rebates. If they are willing to deduct it from the invoice at time of delivery that would be even better.

NOTES

NOTES

OTHER P&L ITEMS

In later chapters we will review other P&L cost cutting measures but we have now covered the two greatest controllable costs on your P&L. The next item will be covered in several places in this book. It is sales and what we can do for immediate sales improvement. The sales line drives the entire P&L. As sales go up then the cost lines naturally fall into place.

You may have heard the line; Sales cure everything! This is not always the case! We are going to solve issues not hide them!

Yes, sales will help cover up problems, but if you have a labor problem to start with then as sales increase chances are the labor problem will follow. Even if the labor line does drop some this is due to salaried management not because the team is now following the schedule or that overtime has gone away. Do not be fooled, or more of your money will be lost. The same applies to cost of goods. If you have a problem it will only worsen even if COGS does drop a little with better sales. Generally this is caused because waste reduces; not because the theft reduces or portioning is correct or for that matter we order any better.

 **The biggest difference you will see as sales increase is the fixed cost percent reduces. What I mean is: rent stays the same as sales go up (unless you have a percent agreement) which can help bottom line profit. Utilities basically stay the same and even labor does not go up as quickly as sales increase so you get disproportionate profit increases to sales increase.**

Later in the book we will review cutting costs on utilities, insurance, alarms, trash, and more. These are on the most part fixed cost items and as sales increase they stay the same. Reducing these items will immediately increase your profit!

NOTES

NOTES

UNSEEN ISSUES/ SETTING GOALS

If you do not have written goals for what you plan to achieve then please take a minute and do so now. You must have a map on where you think you should be. Sales, COGS, labor, all fixed costs, as well as growth plans should be included. A vacation to get away and to drive toward. This is very important for your future. Write these goals down and modify them as need be but stick to getting them done.

 A goal is nothing unless it is written down and followed through! Read it daily and let your goals help focus you on your future! Make a wish list. If I had all the money I needed I would buy: a plane, car, house, boat, or travel. Visualize yourself doing these things and it will help drive you toward your goals!

Look for unseen issues in your place of business. It could be cost cutting or it may be service oriented. i.e. A new product that a customer recommends, added seating, a little paint, or maybe new uniforms to freshen the place. Let everyone know they are part of the solution to growing the business. Share the numbers with key members. If they know where the goal is they will be much more likely to help you get there. Get feedback from not only customers but also your employees. Visit competitors on a regular basis and see what they are doing. Go during peak busy time and see what is being ordered. Do you carry this item? Is theirs better? Have you even taken the time to sample the product to decide?

There are answers to every business problem. We must all open our eyes to see them. Every person you deal with in your business has potential to help you be more successful. Often the best ideas come from the oddest places. Never discount input and ideas!

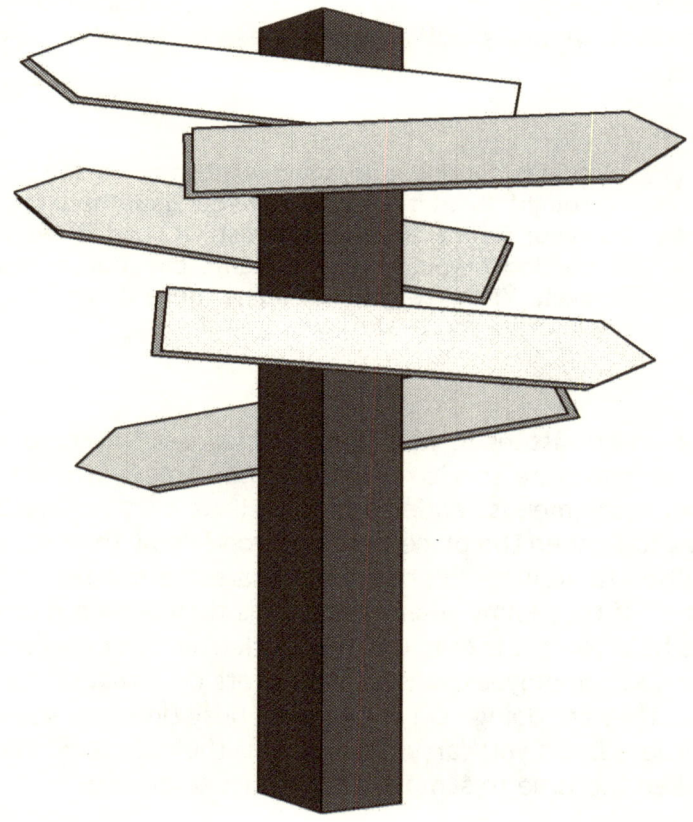

As you continue on in the book more windows of opportunity will arise. Being focused on your business and your customers will answer most questions. Visiting your competition will answer others. Listening to your vendors is another opportunity for help. Set your goals and use all these tools to grow and thrive in your business.

NOTES

NOTES

CUTTING COST TO INCREASE PROFIT

1 Finding Quick Cash

2 Additional Savings

3 Cost of Goods and Inventory

4 Labor/ OT

5 Theft/ Waste

6 Waste

FINDING QUICK CASH

You find yourself in a bind for cash. Bills are due and you either are short on cash to pay or are late. This happens in almost every business at one time or another. What we are going to look for are quick ways to help cash control. Ways that you control so you can move as fast as you choose.

 **Try to react prior to getting behind with your bills. Keep your line of communications open at all times with your accounts payable on your ability to pay or not to pay on a timely basis.**

Let's start with rent. It is one of the highest costs in most businesses. Rent is right up there with the big two: Food and Labor. Landlords want you to succeed for two reasons: they care and to reduce the hassle of having to find a new renter. Finding a new tenant is costly and time consuming. This is very much in your favor. Landlords will not let on that they are as flexible as they really are. They also will go out of their way not to commit to helping until they feel you have done everything else possible to make the business work. Do not be surprised if you have two or even three meetings before the point is driven home. During this time try everything you can do to not get behind on payments. If the Landlord sees that you are trying to work it out they will be much more receptive to waiving fees or even moving the due date.

When you set your first meeting you need to be prepared. Set up the meeting in advance. Do not just show up! Not only is this unprofessional but they will wonder why you have so much time on your hands when you are struggling in business. It sends a message of being out of control. This will carry over to the belief you are spending money unwisely and the Landlord will be difficult to bargain with.

Items to bring to the meeting; bring two copies of each item so you can give the landlord a copy as you review each item:

1. At least three months Profit & Loss Statements. One page each, clear honest numbers. This is the same document you would use for paying tax at the end of the year.

2. A list of all the things you have done already to help the business, for instance; reviewed hours of operation to cut cost and build sales, met with vendors for new products to be introduced to build sales, started a suggestion box for the customers to give feedback. All of these are building the business steps and will show you are concerned and are doing everything you can to turn the business around. This list should be 6-8 items with space for notes after each item.

3. A list of items you are still working on, i.e. meeting with vendors to cut costs, meeting with vendors for help in advertising, meeting with the utility company reference cutting costs. This list should have 8-10 items with a space to make note after each item.

4. The last page concerns creative suggestions for lowering your rent and why. Here are some ideas to try. Customize these for your particular situation:

    • Suggest 6 months to turn the business during which time you pay anywhere from zero rent up to 50% rent. Offer to extend the lease the 6 months on the end of the lease to make up the free rent time by adding the reduced amount to the base rent.

    • Suggest a significant reduction in rent and the amount you reduce the rent by will then be spread evenly over the remainder of the lease. Example would be 6 months at 50% rent. Let's use a base rent of $3,000 a month. Your rent would be reduced for 6 months to $1,500 a month. All total you would have saved $9,000 during that timeframe. The remaining 4 and ½ years your rent would be the base of $3,000 plus $167 for the rent you had reduced for getting your feet under you. Most landlords will agree to this situation since they lose nothing.

- The last suggestion is ask for the rent to be reduced because the sales are not what you had projected them to be. This is tough to get done but if you are sincere on your request and have numbers to show where you stand there is the chance they will allow this.

The Landlord will recognize sincerity. If you show up late for the meeting or are not prepared then you have little or no chance. Your long term success is also your landlords success. A reduction today to reap benefits for a longer period makes good business sense. Sell this with a presentation that shows a long term plan for success and a win/ win situation for you both. You are selling yourself and your belief that you know what you are doing running your business. Provide several copies of your documents so everyone will have their own copies as well as one extra. This way notes can be taken on your documents and they will still have a clean copy for files or for a supervisor.

NOTES

NOTES

ADDITIONAL SAVINGS:

Suppliers:

Another place to find cash is with your suppliers. Again the key is do not get behind and then talk to them. Let them know things are tight and you want to know if you can get terms of 30 days to pay invoices. This will buy time but long term remember you still have those invoices. You need to get cash flow at this point until all the saving items are in place and sales have been increased. This is a stopgap for that timeframe.

Banker:

Next go to visit your bank. A bank today may seem impersonal but if you are a business banking customer and you make the first step of meeting and befriending your banker he/she will go a long way to help you. Bankers know that at times there are cash flow problems in most businesses. It could be related to seasonal issues or even weather conditions. It maybe that every first of the month all the bills are due and it is just a tight time of the month. If you make the banker aware of your issues he will be more likely to keep tabs on your account and give you a call if the account is short instead of sending back your check. It is possible for him to waive certain fees or change billing dates. The next time you stop at your branch office make a point of greeting everyone. Go out of your way to be neighborly and see what happens. After you start doing this, they will look forward to you stopping by. Business owners need a banker who cares!

Further thoughts regarding finding cash and cash flow. Go to your bank that you have your business account with. Request to visit a loan officer. Hopefully you know him/ her and are comfortable sitting down and explaining the situation. Be very up front with where you stand. Let him know you have a cash flow problem right now but you are well on your way to having yourself back on track. Ask him if the bank has a business draw line of credit. This is an account that you actually never touch but is available if you run short and a check needs to clear. This is ideal for those high bill times once a month. It gives you some space to build your business without worrying about if you have enough money to pay the invoices. The loan will not charge you anything unless you use it and then it is similar to an overdraft protection. There will be a monthly payment if the account does have a draw against it, usually a very low amount. The key is try not to use it but if you do pay it back every month. It builds great credit for your future needs and it also does not put you a financial bind.

 Your banker is a friend and a very valuable business partner, get to know him!

Utilities:

Place a call to the utility companies next. Again the key is do not get way behind then call. There are many programs that may help. You may need them to move the billing cycle so it falls at a different time of the month. They may have test programs for new meters or regulator that you can let them install and they will give you a reduction on your bill. There are many tools they have that will further reduce your costs so just ask. Do not spend too much time on this if the person is not helpful. Thank him anyway and hang up. Then call back. There is a very good chance you will get someone else. If you do not; then nicely ask for a supervisor. Explain you have a problem and would feel more comfortable discussing it with a supervisor. Let him know it is not he that is the problem but you. If he feels threatened by you it will have hurt your cause. He will sway the supervisor before even getting them on the phone.

NOTES

NOTES

COST OF GOODS AND INVENTORY

We have spent quite a bit on time in Chapter 1 reference COGS or cost of goods sold. Usually the biggest cost for a business is involved in merchandise. Many businesses make the mistake of carrying too much inventory. Instead of the money being available for paying bills it is sitting on the shelf gathering dust or worse yet spoiling or going out of date. Every time I visit a business that has asked me to give them a review we always get around to discussing inventory and every time I am told "I only order what I need". I then take the time to review reports that show what they sell by product. This is called a product mix report. If you do not use one of these you need to start. It is a simple report that tracks how many of each item you order and how many you sell. This form will also track waste for you so you can reduce products that do not sell. Once you know what you sell then you are ready to work on ordering correctly.

As per earlier you need to have an order guide that suits you not the vendor. Make your own in the order that most suits your location and needs.

Tip: Always group items in categories like: frozen, refrigerated, cups/lids, bags, etc. Then set your store up to match this form. You store will look better and be more organized plus you will reduce labor because items will be grouped and it will take less time to find.

I strongly believe a good order is not possible without doing a good inventory. An inventory gives you the on hand amount of each product. You then refer to your par level. The minimum level needed for each product for a given period of time. Once you get your store set up correctly then this will only take a few minutes to count. A proper order will only be enough product to cover the time from when the order with be dropped off to the next order drop off. You should never carry more than 10% over your projected usage. You are now ready to fill out your order. Look at each item and verify what is on hand then subtract that from what your par level is and that is your order.

Never Never Never fill out your order from behind a desk. You must always walk the store and verify items on hand! I have seen too many orders that were made from either behind a desk or while the person was not in the store. They thought they remembered what they needed! Ha!!!

Another benefit of the correct order is you will never run out of a product. Many incorrect orders turn into a product shortage, which hurts business. The results of this happening is then an over order on the next delivery. It happens all the time and both are not beneficial. One causes you to lose customers, which is our lifeblood while the other puts money on the shelf instead of in the bank.

Significant reduction in costs will benefit from doing this program. You will see a more controlled inventory on the shelf and provide better customer service because you will not run out of products. You can expect at least a 10% decrease in your order by following this program.

Nice little find of some cash on hand! Cash Flow is the key!!

Doing an inventory is a process that is too often taken for granted. There is a great deal of money tied up in inventory yet we put little emphasis on counting and organizing the products. There is a manner to inventory that will guarantee you never have a bad count or miss any items. It is a step-by-step process that when followed will give you a very accurate count which will help you reduce your cost of goods. How will it reduce cost of goods you ask?

1. Fewer products on the shelf mean less product to drop or spill.

2. Fewer products mean less spoilage if a cooler fails or if a product is date coded.

3. Less product results in less theft because if an item is missing and you do not make it through the week you have a very good idea it was taken.

4. Less product means better inventory because items are not hidden from view.

5. Last but not least, less product means your portioning must be better so you do not run out before hitting your projection.

You will receive all of these benefits just from a correct inventory count. As I mentioned it is a set manner to count a store and if followed your counts will always be correct. Here are the steps to a perfect inventory. If you follow every step every time you do inventory you will reduce on unnecessary and improve your cash flow!

1. The same person does the inventory every time it is done.

2. The same person who inventories should place the order for more products.

3. Do the inventory either before the location is open or after it is closed. After closing is the best since there is no rush to complete the inventory to get open.

4. Have a clipboard with the inventory worksheet and two pens to write with and a calculator. Having these on hand will keep you moving and create a better count.

5. Once the inventory is started then stop for nothing. Inventory day should never be on a day when there is a delivery. During inventory take no phone calls, no breaks, answer no questions. This is total focus on one thing and that is an accurate count.

6. To begin always start at the same spot in the location at the same time. For example, you place you order on Monday morning. Every Sunday night after close then do inventory. I like to start at the back door but the point is always start in the same spot every single time.

7. Go either right or left but again always head the same direction. Start counting with the first item on the top shelf all the way on the left and work you way across that shelf. Do not bounce around. Do one shelf at a time then go on to the next. If an item is stored in more than one spot then you should have two or three inventory entries. Do not go and find the product but stay focused on one shelf at a time from left to right top to bottom.

8. Work around the location until you have made a big circle and end up where you started. Every cabinet, shelf, cooler, and closet should have all been counted in the same manner.

9. Now sit down and take a few minutes break. This is the first break since you began and it may take some time depending on your location, size and amount of inventory.

10. Your break is over and now go on to the final step. Add all the items that had more than one storage point. Cups, lids, napkins, are some items that will usually have multiple storage points. Now get your order guide and fill in the on hand for each item.

That's it...you just completed the best inventory count you have ever done!!!!!!

After two or three inventories you will start to move items to a smarter storage point. You will reduce the number of items stored in multiple locations. You will also come across items that you do not use anymore and are just storing.

There are only two places an item should be stored. The first is in it's correct slot on a shelf or in a cooler. The second is if the item is no longer used it goes in the trash. Do not store items not used. It clutters the location, is in the way for inventory, and takes the place of space you can use for items you need! The other issue is the Health Department hates to see out of date items and when you are just storing items this can happen. Don't get dinged for unused items. Throw them away!

You are now ready to place your order. You have an accurate on hand count and an accurate par level. Subtract these two and you have your order for each item. In this manner you will significantly reduce inventory and costs.

A quick note on receiving your order and being prepared. Have ample staff on hand so you can check in the order without interruption. Second make sure all stock has been rotated so the stocking will be easy. Third always have your order guide on a clipboard to compare to the actual invoice. Look for price changes and completeness. Last have a magic marker. As every box comes in put a big check on the box and then check it off on your invoice. This is a double check system that guarantees you have seen every item on the invoice. After you check everything in then date each box as you but the item away. Even non perishable items. This helps to see how fast you are turning your stock. It also helps to make sure you are rotating products so they stay fresh and you have less spoilage. What you will find is dates that will help you know how often you need to order an item. Again, this reduces on hand stock. You may find a half case of cups lasts a week but you have been ordering a case anyway.

Hold off on ordering as you find this information out. You have great potential of loss when you buy something and it sits on your shelf too long. Keep your money in the bank!!!

NOTES

NOTES

LABOR/OT

Labor is the easiest item to control and track. Having said this labor is the most abused item in most situations. Thousands of dollars every month fly out the door from not controlling your labor. Here are some of the ways you lose money:

1. Employees clocking in early.

2. Employees clocking out late.

3. Employees working more than 40 hours a week.

4. When business is slow not sending employees on unpaid breaks.

5. When business is slow not sending employees home early.

6. Employees clocking in then heading to the bathroom to get ready. Employees should be ready to work when they clock in.

7. Do not allow employees to take breaks without clocking out.

8. Over scheduling your employees.

9. Not having a plan if weather is inclement.

10. Not having a daily, hourly, weekly goal.

These are all easy to deal with but they almost never get fixed. It is a day in and day out job to control labor. You are dealing with people who want and need the money, but do not realize the responsibility of controlling labor costs.

Let's do a little example of some labor situations:

You have 10 employees.
Average wage is $7.00 per hour.
Each employee is to work 35 hours a week.

Your payroll will be: $2,450
10 employees X 35 hours X $7.00 hour
You project your sales to be $8,000.

Your labor percent will be 30.6% $2,450 divided by $8,000

The end of the week comes around and here is what was clocked in:

1.	37 hours	Clocking early/ staying late
2.	36 hours	Clocking early/ staying late
3.	42 hours	Filled in for employee
4.	29 hours	Called in
5.	38 hours	Clocking early/ staying late
6.	47 hours	Stayed late because couldn't find a ride
7.	32 hours	Clocking early/ staying late
8.	39 hours	Rode with the person who couldn't find a ride
9.	41 hours	Stayed late every shift 1 hour
10.	35 hours	

Now let's figure payroll and see where we end up:

Total hours paid are 376 instead of 350. This is not many but let's see what the cost is to you. You have 10 hours overtime paid at time and a half.

366 X $7 hour equal	$2,562
10 X $10.50 hour	$105
TOTAL ACTUAL	$2,667

Over spent   **$217**

Sales were right on at $8,000 so your labor percent was 33.3%
$2,667 divided by $8,000.

Now let's use this as the average throughout the year.

SALES   *$8,000 A WEEK FOR 52 WEEKS*   *$416,000*
LABOR ACTUAL   *$2,667 A WEEK FOR 52 WEEKS*   *$138,684*
LABOR PLANNED   *$2,450 A WEEK FOR 52 WEEKS*   *$127,400*

Lets double the costs for a higher volume situation and compare also:

SALES   *$16,000 A WEEK FOR 52 WEEKS*   *$832,000*
LABOR ACTUAL   *$5,334 A WEEK FOR 52 WEEKS*   *$277,368*
LABOR PLANNED   *$4,900 A WEEK FOR 52 WEEKS*   *$254,800*

That means there was an over spending of **$11,284** in the low volume unit and **$22,568** in the higher volume in labor. Businesses cannot handle that kind of cost. The above is a low average in the restaurant industry. Actually when you do this calculation in your location you may find it much worse.

The key to great labor is a great schedule and following this schedule under all circumstances. Do not allow employees to stay over or clock in early. Always know who is about to have overtime and send them home.

The only time you need to keep someone overtime is if it would hurt your ability to serve your customer!

Take the time to make a great schedule. You do not need to change it every week. Put your best team on when you have the most business. Make sure everyone knows there is no clocking in early or staying late. Never ever schedule someone into overtime.

The best thing to do is never schedule anyone over 35 hours. This gives you five hours of room if someone calls in that you can use to cover the shift. Once you get a great schedule let everyone give you feedback. If the team knows you want them happy and they understand why they cannot stay over they will help you. Also if you work the schedule around school and use the same schedule week after week the team can make plans to take care of their personal things on their day off. The more notice you give of when people are to work the better they will feel and the more likely they will show up. This will also help reduce turnover because people like a workplace they feel a part of making a win/ win situation for the entire team!

NOTES

NOTES

THEFT/WASTE

By doing a great inventory and better organizing your location you have already gone a long way to reducing theft and waste. The number one theft in the food industry is not money, it's food. Examples of food theft may be: food eaten, given to friends, given to family, or even taken out the backdoor for home use. You have now done the first step in reducing this problem. Less inventory means any item missing is more likely to be noticed. The next step, and it is almost as important, is to have a very clear policy as to who gets free products, discounted products, and how much of the product they can have at either a discount, or free. Ignorance to the policy is one of the largest causes to food theft.

 **Always be consistent to the policy. This includes yourself, your friends, and your family. Set the example and by doing so you will make it clear how things are to be handled.**

To stop theft, always have boxes broken down flat prior to ever opening the door to take out the trash. Always send two people to handle the trash. If something were taken they would have to split it and usually that would not be worth the risk. The last item to reduce theft of products is called a critical count inventory. Pick

4 or 5 products that have either high cost or are easy to transport or could be used easily at home. Daily count these items at every open and every close. If you have a shift change; count again. It will only take a couple minutes to count. What you will find is that people will notice you counting and be less likely to chance taking anything. The other thing is that you will have let everyone know who worked on what shift when the item came up missing. The entire group will then help you watch out for each other.

The goal is to remove temptation. People overall are not thieves but don't tempt them to become one!

Cash theft is a different matter. Without a great deal of cost to you I will give several ways to reduce cash shortage issues.

The first way is to never have more than one person use a cash register at a time. Hold one person 100% accountable the their drawer. When they go on break lock the drawer up. If you have only one register then count it down and when they return let them do another task.

There is no cash control possible if people share a register!!!

Remove all twenties and excess bills from the cash drawer every half hour. Don't leave enough in the drawer to tempt your employees. This is also good for security measures. Let your employees know that is one of the reasons for pulling cash so often. Have an envelope for each cashier and have him or her sign what you pulled then drop it in your safe. If you do not have a safe then lock it in a desk but always secure the money out of sight. At the end of the shift always have the cashier count down the drawer with you. They should never do it alone and neither should you. Always praise when they are correct, say plus or minus $1 for the shift. If over, then there is a good chance they were going to steal. If short, then they may either have a problem counting, giving incorrect change or stealing.

A great deterrent to stealing is to do spot drawer audits. Pick a time in mid shift and change cashiers. The cashier you pull will then go with you and you both will count down their drawer. A surprise audit will be a major deterrent to theft in the future. If there is a shortage or overage you need to audit your own safe and verify, if correct then call the Police. This is setting a major example that theft will not be tolerated.

I have mentioned twice cash being over. This is called building the bank. It means that the cashier is slowly under charging the customer or is shortchanging the customer. Money does not grow. You have cash come in and product go out. It must balance or there is a problem. One sign someone is building the bank is if you see change being left in a slot not where it belongs. For example, you open the drawer and see several dimes, nickels, and pennies in a slot all the way to the left of the drawer where fifty-cent pieces should go. Ask the cashier why they have done this and a typical response will usually be; "I was trying to hurry because we were busy, I'll put it in the right slots now." Instead immediately pull the drawer and do a count. Yes; it is possible they were telling the truth but in reality it takes only seconds to slot the coin correctly.

In building a bank the thief will use coins to let them know how much bank they have built. A dime is $10, a nickel is $5, and a penny is $1. Rarely quarters mean anything except to help them look innocent as well as four quarters and they have another dollar.

 **The key to reducing bank building is audit regularly and stay out of the back room. Management people need to interact with the customer regularly. Your being cautious is a great precaution.**

A security camera is a helpful tool but unless you have hundreds of dollars for very good equipment it will help little. Bad picture quality and the need for multiple cameras drives the cost too high for most businesses. You can find reasonable cost fake cameras that will deter some thieves but as mentioned above the best deterrent is to remove temptation and make getting caught costly.

NOTES

NOTES

WASTE

Waste is not only an issue of leftover product to be discarded. Waste is any item that was to be used to produce income that does not do so. Paper falling on floors, cups employees drink from, overfilling napkin containers so they tear when customers try to remove them from the dispenser, too many condiments given out, and even over portion are all examples.

All these result in higher cost of goods. The greater the focus on details the greater the profitability of your business and in turn increase in equity. Be aware of items dropping on the floor. Get everyone aware of how much it costs then compare it to throwing money away. People understand when they hear; "That cup cost $.25 that just hit the floor. Would you stop and pick up a quarter if you saw one on the floor?" The answer will be a yes, and then you have made the point. Cups are money, be careful. Set a standard for items given out. How many napkins per order, ketchup, mustard, etc. for all items. The customer will appreciate not having to ask for these items and at the same time they will not get more than they need. Everyone wins in this program.

Portioning is a two-fold issue. Under portion causes you bad quality and causes you to lose business, over portion causes high cost of goods and can also result in bad quality. In every work station there should be a chart explaining the portion for each item produced or served. These are reminders to help everyone focus on portion, which in turns reduces cost and builds business. Items as simple as ice for a soda should be on the list. With too little ice, not only is there too much soda, but the ice melts quicker and waters down the drink and creates bad quality. Too much ice and the customer feels cheated and will go elsewhere.

 Small cards laminated for the employee's pockets are a help. Once they are assigned a position give them a position card. It will have job responsibility, product portion information, as well as any duty to be completed at shift end. This frees the management team up to interact with the customer and to monitor other things such as cash and quality. Time is money!!!

NOTES

NOTES

LONG TERM SUCCESS

1 Vendor Relationship

2 Building Business Equity

3 Listen

4 Adjust as Need

VENDOR RELATIONSHIP

I cannot express enough on how important your relationship is with your vendors. You are the customer and usually you can find another vendor if need be but it is much better to work together with the vendor. Do not treat them with anything but respect and appreciation. There will be bumps in the road and it is much easier to repair them with good relations. Vendors have the power to offer help with product cost, new product introduction, rebates, advertising, and many other things. There is the ability to get payment terms set up. This is key for cash flow at certain times of the month and year. New products to help build your business can be introduced on a regular basis. All this said there is one thing that your vendors can do to help more than anything. They can be your eyes and ears while they travel and do their job.

When a vendor visits your competitor and he sees new products or a new menu or even a business that is going to close he will share this with you if you have a good relationship! This is very powerful information and you may never have found these things out or you may have found out too late!

If a store near you is closing then it will directly affect the amount of business you have in your location. With this in mind and the fact they are new customers you need to have extra product available. Never run out or that is what they will remember. Have an extra staff person working to make sure you have great service even if you get very busy. Go out of the way to let everyone know you want their business and you are there to serve them.

New products that a competitor has introduced can hurt your sales. You could lose customers and not even know why. On the other end of that thought would be for you to introduce new products on a regular basis so you constantly let the customer know you are flexible and want to have a menu they want. With good vendor relationships you will find out about products early on or even price increases that will take effect. There will be the opportunity for the vendor to partner with you to grow your business. This is a win/ win situation. You grow and increase sales and they get added purchases from you.

Spend the time to grow this relationship. Take time to visit with your vendors on a monthly basis, one on one. Don't always wait for them to come to you; call them and set up a meeting. Offer to do product testing for new products. They pay for these items and will supply free advertising for you. Remember win win situation!

BUILDING BUSINESS EQUITY

The goal of a business is to grow. If you are not growing then chances are you will not survive. Rents increase, utilities increase, labor cost increases, and also product cost increases. For a while you can cover up the lack of sales growth with price increase. Long term you must grow top line sales to survive. Business equity is increased through growth more than any single factor. The faster you grow for the longer the period the greater your equity. Nothing will affect the value of your business more than a healthy sales growth line. The fixed costs can only eat up so much of the profits until the remainder falls to the net profit line.

Keep this in mind as you trend sales. If you are just maintaining then you are losing value. For every action there is a like reaction. You do not want to wait to react, you want to act.

By the time you have to react it may be too late. It does not cost a great deal to get your company name out in the community. In the next chapter we will talk about low cost alternatives in advertising. Just remember if you are not growing you are losing equity and eventually your increase in fixed cost will run you out of business. Worse yet is if your sales are sliding and because you still make some money you are in the wait and see mode. As mentioned, do not wait until you have to react; act and act now!

LISTEN

It is a funny thing how little things like listening can help your business thrive. It costs nothing to do but could cost you losing your business. There are ideas and solutions to every situation; not all are yours and that is fine. Your employees are a great resource of ideas. In many cases they have more contact with your customer than you do as the business owner. Make a point to listen to ideas and as your employees find out that you care they will bring more ideas. Let them know how important their ideas can be in the success of the business. Take the time to hear your customers. Are they talking about a new product or maybe the fact a competitor is opening down the street?

 **Maybe you will be the one to invent the next craze in the industry but your odds are better the more people you listen to and learn from. My mother once told me the most brilliant minds in the world belong to those who read the most. It doesn't matter what you read you will learn. All of my life I have read. I try to read a book a week. I know it has helped me to expand my thoughts and to be a more creative businessperson. To see solutions to problems.**

Even if you are a very educated individual there will always be someone with a better idea right behind you. Sharing your knowledge but also taking the time to listen is a big key to ongoing success. Many of the richest people in the world with all the material things they could ever want achieve that position through ideas that were not even their own. They listened, perfected, and then initiated the plan to bring on the success. Most often the person who had the idea originally never understood that they were the inspiration for the idea. It could be a product, a service idea, or maybe even a new location in an area you would never have found.

 The key is to listen and to use this information to help you grow your business and maybe even grow yourself.

ADJUST AS NEEDED

As mentioned several times throughout this book you must react or adjust to customer trend. What is the number one best seller today will not necessarily be tomorrow. As you use your listening skills to learn you need to also act. Whether it is a new product that has hit it big or the need for a spruce up of your location. New landscape is a great way to tell the customer something is new. Fresh trim paint or even some added lights put in trees or along the pathways will help bring attention.

The key is to be able to quickly adjust as the need arises. New products are a great way to keep your business growing.

The key is to be able to act and not to always wait until it's too late and then need to react. Your customer base is dropping. You have no idea why. The product hasn't changed, the place looks the same, and even the employees are the same. Hmmmmmmm. Maybe that IS the problem! People change and you must change with them. Frequently do a new menu for example. Low cost menus are a great way to maintain excitement. Add weekly specials and change food items from week to week. If an item hits it off big then add it to the menu next time you print new menus. Never become so content that you decide there is no need to adjust. Look at the big companies and how often do they have new products. Maybe it is a new kid toy or a movie they sponsor. They are constantly adjusting to needs.

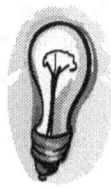 **Be quick to act and you will not have a need to react! Adjust often but also keep your core business the same.**

Never lose sight of what you are in business for **to serve the customer**. You are not in the business to make money and if that is how you are thinking then the customer will figure it out and you will fail! Serve the customer and you will make money, grow your business, and reap the rewards when you sell.

NOTES

NOTES

GREAT SERVICE MEANS GREAT BUSINESS BUILDING SALES

1 Value of Great Service

2 Power of Word Of Mouth

3 Vendor Advertising Help/ Low Cost Solutions

4 Power of L.T.O.'s

VALUE OF GREAT SERVICE

You can have the best product in the best location and still fail. How? Bad service. The root of service is to serve. We must serve our customers or they will go somewhere else. There is no product that cannot be duplicated. There is another location on every corner and on more than one corner many times that want your business. A fancy store will only keep the customer so long and even great product will only keep the customer so long. Then you will hit advertising hard and that too will dry up and quit bringing in the customer. The one thing that will keep customers coming back over and over again is service. To let every customer know that our one goal is to serve their needs while they are in our store. Nothing is more important than that one single thought. Ironically this is the greatest failure in business today.

Service is spoken of but very rarely followed up on in a regular manner. Policies do not make people give great service; people make people give great service.

Always be the example. Always give a hand even when you are busy with another project. This is the best training you could ever give. Employees will learn more from watching you than from anywhere else. This includes the bad habits, so keep that in mind next time you are too busy to serve a customer. Be the example and coach your team on what is expected for great customer service. Your business will not only survive but also thrive!

This leads me into our next topic.

POWER OF WORD OF MOUTH

The most powerful of advertising campaign will fail if your reputation is bad. The stats say that every time a person has a bad experience they go and tell seven more people who tell 4 more people who tell 3 more people. For that one problem not taken care of you have now involved over 30 people. Imagine if this happens every single day. Your whole town will know in weeks and you will be out of business. No customer should ever leave your location without having their problem resolved to their satisfaction. No matter what it takes there is always a way.

 The quickest way to diffuse a bad situation is apologize. It is hard to stay mad when the first words you tell them are; "I am so sorry for _____. What can I do to make you happy?"

By the time they leave even if the product is given to them they are happy and will return. You cared to serve them and your reward is a return visit. Not only a return visit but also they will probably bring friends since they feel you cared so much. Word of mouth advertising is a double-edged sword. It can deal a crushing blow or can be the most powerful advertising media available anywhere. Bad service, product, and/ or a situation and you will be driven out of business. Great service, product, and environment you will flourish. I do not mean this lightly in any way. In many businesses there is little money to advertise. You need people to talk about your business.

Every chance you get to interact you help create an environment that will drive business to you. The hairdresser visits and has a great time. Wonderful product and the best service he or she has every had anywhere. How many people will this person share that with? Who really knows but the exact opposite could reach 30 people for a bad complaint. That is powerful advertising.

 **No matter what it takes never let a customer leave prior to resolving a complaint. If you did not know that there was a problem and they call you, then let them know how sorry you are and invite them back for a chance to sit down with you and talk. A free meal goes a long way and your sincere caring will go even further. You must stop the spread of problems before they spread.**

Every person on your workforce must have the ability to resolve any problem. If you are not available they must know that they can do anything up to and including give the product away free. After the customer has left, then resolve why the problem happened and what could you have done differently to not let it ever happen again. This is when training and reinforcement come into play to put in place a long-term solution.

 A last thought on word of mouth is you could greatly reduce your advertising costs as well as the discounts given if you get into the habit of keeping customers happy.

 Advertising is a way to buy back the customer you had but ran off for one reason or another. Don't lose the customer in the first place and save the cost!

VENDOR ADVERTISING HELP/ LOW COST SOLUTIONS

Most small businesses have no idea the amount of help they can get from their vendors. The vendors will not tell you nor will they even suggest they can help you. You must ask. Have a plan as to what you want and then approach the vendor or vendors with your idea. The vendors all have a budget just for the asking to help you advertise and grow your business. They in turn sell you more goods so everyone wins. The problem is only the big businesses are aware of this money so they get the lions share. You can even use two or three vendors to pay for an entire marketing piece. Usually all you have to do is explain what you want to do, for instance a direct mail piece. Tell them you would like them to participate and you will put their product name/ photo and logo on the mailer. You need to already know how much this ad will cost so you can tell them. The first goal is to get them committed on how great the idea is and they need to help out. Not too tough, once you have them hooked, so to speak, and then you go for free product. Perhaps the product you are going to advertise is chicken tenders. Let them know you want to sample the product plus you are going to offer a deep discount on the mailer. Last but not least, if all goes well you plan on putting it on your new menu.

 Let's see what you have just accomplished. The ad will be at little or no cost to you. You will get free product which means you will have very low cost tied up. And last but not least you will increase sales because your advertising will be deeply discounted.

This is happening every single day for the major corporations. You deserve your piece of the pie and now it is time to take it. Continuing with that same train of thought about chicken tenders. The ad was a big success and everyone is happy. You call the vendor back for a follow up meeting. Of course you rave how great everything went and that you plan on putting the product on your menu permanently. The vendor is happy. He or she is ready to take your next order right then. "Not quite yet:, you say. There is the cost factor involved and if you sell a great deal of the product would the vendor consider reducing the price per case. The first response will be confusion on the vendors part as to how you knew you could ask them for the reduction. The next response will be a few cents a case. Ask for a rebate of at least $1 per case off the delivered price. Case cost $28 to your door and you will either be invoiced at $27 or at the end of each quarter you will get a check in the mail for what equals to $1 off each case you have bought. Do this same process again after you get the $1 and ask for a small ad fee to come out of the cost so that you and the vendor can run another ad in a few months. You should be able to easily get $.50 per case for ad money. This money is to only be used for future advertising and agree you will not get the money if you do not advertise.

 **In a twenty to thirty minute meeting you received a cash rebate or case cost reduction. You also have an ad fund being set aside to further help grow your business and all you had to do was ask! Remember; you know now that this is available to you, now you need to get it working for you. What a great concept- free money to advertise as well as either greatly reduced product cost or free products and all of this to help build your sales thereby growing your bottom line just by asking!**

Let's have a little more fun with the vendor. Let them know you want to have this great product as a focus product. It needs added marketing in the location to help build sales. These marketing kits for you to have made would cost you hundreds of dollars and some items would be so costly you would never have them available. They will have these kits. Table art, window art, hanging posters, perhaps even neon. Inflatable balloons and employee pins, can be all free to you for just asking. People love to read items sitting on tables and this is free for you so get it rolling!

NOTES

NOTES

POWER OF L.T.O.'S

An L.T.O. is short for limited time offer. You see it all the time. A sandwich is only available for one month. A special cup or toy is available for only for a short time. This is to create urgency for the customer to rush into the location and buy. Most L.T.O.'s are actually menu tests as we mentioned above doing. Heavily backed by free ad money and free or low cost product. This is how a $2.99 chicken sandwich can be sold for $1.00. They get the meat free so they can afford to do the promotion.

You can run an L.T.O. at a premium price also. This has the same rush in urgency goal, but if the cost is too high the repeat business will not happen. The best L.T.O.'s seem to always end up on the menu. This tells you the product sold well and they expect it to maintain. An L.T.O. is a great quick hit you can run every month. It can be run at little or no cost to you, many times with very low product cost, and advertising paid by someone else.

While meeting with your vendors you will meet with their product representatives. These people have several different brands they represent. You may be meeting about ketchup and they bring up a new snack idea or a new cup suggestion. Always allow them to show you new items and always get them to bring in samples for you to test. If you feel good about them but are not ready to run an ad or an L.T.O. then ask them for several cases for you to test in store. Get window clings/ posters and some table tents and try the product out. The best new products will: bring in new customers, drive higher check average, or add a whole new line of products to increase spending. Ice cream is a great example that does this. If you do not have a dessert line, then bringing in ice cream offers your customer a sweet treat after the meal. It has no competition inside your location since you sell no desserts. You are basically taking that business away from the shop down the street that your customers visit after eating dinner with you.

 An L.T.O. can be a very powerful low cost method to test menu products prior to spending the money to print menus. You can project what you can expect in sales and also can gear up for this to be a permanent menu item.

NOTES

NOTES

REDUCING OVERHEAD

1 Landlord Negotiations

2 Utilities

3 Insurance Company

4 Misc: Alarms, Trash, Exterminator,
   Linen/Towels/aprons, Music

LANDLORD NEGOTIATIONS

I will expand our earlier review of landlord costs and how you can negotiate a better financial situation.

The key to any negotiation is to have a plan. An outcome that you want and even decide must have prior to making a deal. Landlords have a goal of getting market value for each of their properties. Your goal should be to pay the absolute least you have to pay while still getting the space you want.

 **Prior to meeting with the landlord you need to do some homework. Without doing this you will never achieve the best possible situation.**

1. You must find out what the going rate per square foot for the area you are interested in moving into. Not just from the property you are interested but all properties in the area.

2. Next you need to know how many vacancies there are in the area.

3. How long have these properties been vacant?

4. The space you have interest in is empty; why? (If you are working to negotiate your present lease then disregard.)

Look at the area you are interested in and look for growth, new centers of activity, road construction. All these tell you if the area is booming or has developed and is now maintaining. These are big factors for Landlords to either raise rent or to start out high. If you know the area will be booming but is not now then you need to plan to get as long a lease as possible keeping the rent in check!

Reasons you think an area will boom in the future: new school or church being planned in area, road being widened or even moved, new facility, any new office space being planned or built.

 **Your success is hinged on you having as much or even more knowledge of the area than your Landlord. The greater your information the easier you can negotiate.**

When you have all the information you feel can be gained in this area from your visits to other tenants and your own observation, then it's time to go to the next step. Go to the local courthouse. Talk to the clerks about the area you are interested in and what you are planning. They have the ability to acquire a great deal of information. This is a step most Landlords will not take the time to review. The clerk will be able to find or to direct you where to find out information. Building permits for any structure in the area. This will give you detailed information on growth, when the growth will happen, size of project, and what kind of growth is in the area. This is powerful information that you can also use in your business plan for projecting future sales and growth potential. As you can imagine if an office is opening next door that will house 5,000 people then you just expanded your customer availability by that same number. The opposite end of this is you may find a competitor is planning on opening a similar type place on the same corner you are. This can have the reverse effect and could potentially drive business away. You will also want to inquire about any possible plan to widen roads in the area since this can effect traffic getting to your place for a period of time. What if the project turns your road into a one way street the wrong way for your business for a year or two? This could close your doors. Also find out about any plan for a median or limited access situation being evaluated. A median can completely alter the traffic pattern and make your potential site a disaster to enter or exit.

Ask as many questions as you must to get this information. Take time with the clerk. They are doing you a favor in providing this information and can directly help you to survive in business. This may not be the only site you look at so befriending this person would benefit in that manner also. It never hurts to be appreciative.

Last thought when visiting the courthouse. The clerk may give you bad news. Don't get upset at the clerk. They may have just saved you a great deal of money in the future. Thank them and even ask them if they know of other potential sites of growth where you could look. They may have just seen where a new development was going in and set you on a goldmine!!!

Now it is time to set the appointment with your potential Landlord or Property Manager. When you call you need to be clear on why you are calling. If you do not have a name of an individual then ask who is the property manager for the property you are interested in. Ask if this person is available. You will probably be asked for your name and even what you are calling in reference to. Tell them you have interest in whatever the property is and would like to meet with the property manager. If you get a voice mail do not leave too much information. You want them to call you and not know details. This gives you an advantage for the first conversation. Just let them know you have interest in a property they manage and ask them to call you back. Leave your name and number and that is enough. If you get put straight through then have your notes handy for any off-the-cuff question you may be asked but overall you DO NOT want to negotiate in any way over the phone. You want to meet person to person. The sole purpose is to set up a meeting and to let the Landlord know of your interest in a specific space. You will need to disclose the business type but details are not necessary.

The goal is to set a meeting and not negotiate over the phone. The management company feels much more power behind the phone line than they usually are in person. They are just like you and use the structure of being with a management company as a power tool. Relax; you are the customer and they need to get you to rent the space!

Once the meeting is set then you need to compile your notes in brief bullet point statements. You will need to bring your financial statement, projected sales reports, and your notes. The more prepared you are going into this first meeting, the better the chance you will get a favorable lease. Here is an example order to direct the conversation:

1. Start with getting them to tell you about the center as to age, future growth plans, empty spaces and how long they have been unoccupied. Try to feel if this person is going to share openly about this information. You will already know much of what they are going to tell you. This is key to know later if they are just looking to fill the vacancy or if they are looking for a fit for the center with a planned change.

2. Ask specifics on the space of interest. What was there? Why did they close? Did they relocate to another center? These are key questions because they could lead to a problem. Was the rent too high? Was there not enough traffic? Again, you will know some of this information but right now you are still testing the waters.

3. Ask about any large space renter in the center. Does the management company know of any businesses moving out of their center? The larger the business the greater the concern.

4. Get them to talk about traffic count within the lot over the past few months and compared to last year. Is it higher or lower? They may balk at giving you too much detail and try to avoid answering by saying they will have to look it up and will get back to you. This is clearly a ploy to hope you forget to ask again and probably means counts are dropping. All centers track car count. Do not let them lead you on. If they refuse or claim they don't have a car count then you need to think twice about renting from them. If they refuse that information what else will they do that is wrong?

5. Now is the time to get more specific. Overview your business plan. Do not at this point share any projected sales numbers!!!!! Talk about how you choose this business, how long you may have been in this field, how many employees you will hire, and give

only an overview. Cover any specifics that could draw concern which will effect the center. An example would be taking too many parking places from other renters or staying open very late and this could promote vandalism. Discuss openly a plan and the management company will understand. If you are not prepared then there will be a red flag. This could cause your rent to be higher, cause you to have a very high deposit, or even cause them to not let you rent at all.

6. It has now reached money time. How much per square foot are they asking for the space you are interested in? If there are multiple spaces then ask about the uses for all of them. As stated, you should already know how much some of the others spaces are paying. Knowledge is power in this point in a big way. You must know what others are paying to have any idea if you are being taken advantage of or if they are being fair. You also must have already decided what you can afford to pay. Your business plan should have a budget figure for rent. This is your "high water mark". You should never go higher than you have projected as to what you can afford.

7. Once you have a figure then comes the negotiating part. Always open with letting them know that whatever figure they gave you is higher than you projected! Even if it is about mark as to what you thought the key is, they do not know this. Use your acting skills to look worried! Mention you are very interested in the area but are not sure the number will work. At this point you will probably be offered the option of a long term lease at a slightly lower square foot cost. Instead of 5 years then you will be offered 5 years with a 5 year extension at the end. During the 10 year term you will have slight increases in square foot cost every couple years. Depending on how much you save up front and whether you are very confident the area will grow is your decision to agree to this lease.

8. I will close negotiating out with several other items you can ask for and many times will receive if properly negotiated. Again the key is knowledge. Did any other renter get any of these items?

- Ask for up to 6 months rent free so you can establish your business upon opening.

- Request money to help build out the space up front. This would cover items that will stay even if you leave. Air conditioning unit, wall covering, flooring, lights, vent hoods, bathroom fixtures, plumbing and or electrical wiring. Most centers will pick up part of the cost and set the figure depending on length of lease and square foot used.

- Request designated parking for your space. This is very important in an area where parking is tight!

- Request free parking for you and your employees if the area is paid parking only. Downtown location type situations usually qualify.

- Request that you be able to have banners and signs up for grand opening and special events. This is important to have in the lease since many centers will not allow any temporary signage.

There is a great deal of leg work to complete a good lease. The key is to be prepared and comfortable to ask the right questions! Remember you are the customer and should be treated as such!!

NOTES

NOTES

UTILITIES

When you review your Profit and Loss statement you will find that utilities is one of the highest cost centers. Cost of Goods (supplies), labor, rent, and then utilities. With greater focus you can and will cut your utility costs by at least 10%. This is a tremendous boom to your profit line. With only a few steps you will be on your way to building an immediate long-term reduction in cost which in turn creates profit.

The are several steps to maximizing reduction:

1. Always review your statement each month for errors. Take the 15 to 20 minutes to verify the meter was read correctly. Look to see if there is an unusual spike in usage. This could be caused from overuse, a repair problem, new equipment installed, or an error on the utility company part.

2. Install auto set back AC/Heat controls. These programmable jewels will pay for themselves in a mater of weeks. When setting remember not to set the temp too low in the off hours since it takes time to re-heat or cool the space. This could cause a surge and INCREASE you bill. Set in winter to 68 degrees during open hours and 62 degrees when no one is in the location. During summer set to 78 degrees and 82 during off times. Make sure to buy a box to limit access if the unit is in a non-secured area.

3. Install ceiling fans wherever applicable. A ceiling fan will drop the ambient temperature by up to 10 degrees to the feel of the skin. This mean you can further reduce the temperature generated by your units. Make sure to set the fan to draw air down for summer and up for winter. During winter a fan pulls the cooler air from the floor and forces the warmer trapped air from the ceiling down. Many people fail to see the significant saving by using a fan year around! Most fans use only the energy needed to power a 100-watt light bulb.

4. Have an energy audit. These are provided free of charge from your utility company. They will look for ways to save you energy.

There are also companies that will audit old bills and look for savings. These companies also are called energy auditors and are fee based. Usually they will want 50% of whatever they find on old bills. They will do all the work and if they find any money you overpaid they will request it to be sent. Over 50% of all business have been found to be overpaying. Different industries are charged at different rates. The Power Company is not the one to verify you are charged the right rate...... That is your responsibility. The auditor will find this and verify not only do you get a refund but also going forward you will be billed correctly. Expect this process to take about six weeks to review then another few weeks to get the check in the mail. Remember the Auditor Company will need to be paid!

5. Equipment such as coolers are a huge drain. Propped open doors during delivery or any other time is a waste. Plan to check in your order then open the cooler only long enough to pile in the items. Then enter the cooler if a walk in and organize with the door shut. Never allow the doors to be left open. Next on coolers are the door gaskets. These must be kept in good repair. Tears can cause a door to not close properly and allow a tremendous amount of escaped energy. Even a small rip can allow the cooler to have to overwork to maintain temperature. Never should there be an item available that is used to prop open the door. A broomstick, block, rope, or any other item. These items available tell the employees it is allowed to prop open the doors! Last on coolers is to look at the settings. Make sure you are not setting the coolers too low. If products are to be maintained at 0 degrees then the cooler does not need to be set to run 20 below zero. This is a waste of energy as well as time to allow thawing. While checking the setting check to make sure the coils are clean, service a minimum on annual, and also verify the defrost cycle. Too often or set too long on defrost is a waste. The defrost cycle should only be long enough to melt all the ice from the coils. Once a day set during close times is best. The cooler doors will not be open and shut during that time and the unit will be running the most efficiently. Staying with equipment always keep your equipment maintained. Clean filters, coils, do not block intake or exhaust, gaskets, and even drips all will cost or save you money. The top of a walk-in is not a storage point. You can cause serious damage to the unit as

well as increase your energy usage buy storing items on top of a cooler. Check your hot water heater......... It should not be set to run as hot as possible. Turn it back to the recommend setting. This will reduce energy usage as well as extend the life of the heater. Fryer elements........ Clean them with every filter of your shortening. It takes but a few minutes but will extend the life of the fryer as well as make the unit run more efficiently. Lighting...... Mark all the lights for one of three choices: on always, on at open only, on at night open. Lights left on all the time in office space, employee bathrooms, walk-in coolers, parking lots, etc. all waste a tremendous amount of energy. Take a few minutes and label. Teach your employees which to turn on and off. Turn off at close all equipment except items like coolers and items needed to maintain safety or people or product. Take a few minutes and walk around your location....... What else can you do to reduce equipment utility cost?

6. Make up a checklist for energy savings. The list should have three parts as a minimum. Laminate the sheet and post with each shift. Part one should be for the opener. What to turn on, what order, and when. If the equipment is not all turned on at once your overall bill rate will be reduced. The utility company charges more when a company has large hits or spikes in usage in a given time frame. Turn on one fryer and wait 10 minutes then the next and so forth. This will reduce spikes and reduce your bill. The second part is at open. More lighting will be turned on, the heating and cooling should kick in, cash registers turned on, small equipment depending on your business. The third part will be close. When to turn off equipment, lights, etc. As close nears you may not need all the fryers; shut down all unneeded equipment. Then at close turn down all the close items on your list. This ensures a better close but also reduces the utilities. A double win. You may want to add a section for pre rush or shift change. This sheet would be a great place to record cooler temperatures throughout the day. By adding this to your checklist you are forcing someone to check to make sure the cooler doors are closed but also that they are working. Many times you will find a door not shut completely and if the equipment has stopped working you will be able to save the product thereby reducing cost of goods from waste.

EXAMPLE UTILITY CHECKLIST:

TIME	TO DO	COMPLETED BY
7AM	LIGHTING ON	
715AM	VENT HOOD ON	
730AM	FRYER 1 ON	
8AM	FRYER 2 ON	
815AM	OVEN ON	

ETC.... ALL THE WAY THROUGOUT THE DAY

Then at the end of day it will look like this:

7PM	FRYER 1 OFF	
730PM	LOT LIGHTS ON	
8PM	2ND REGISTER OFF	
830PM	OVEN OFF	
CLOSE	LIGHTING/ 2ND FRYER/ ETC	

Detail the list to fit your needs and teach everyone how important this is and how it will save money and even time. Also, it will help insure a better close which then creates a better open to your next day!!!

7. Drips and running toilets. Hundreds and even thousands of gallons of water every year are wasted from small drips on sinks and running toilets. A dripping faucet wastes as much energy as it takes to light a 100-watt light bulb. If you have several dripping sinks then you may be wasting enough to power your lobby lights. Scary to think of it that way but stop watching the money go down the drain..... Pun intended! Every single time a toilet flushes between 1.5 gallons of water and 5 gallons of water in used. If you have a toilet that leaks and continues to run on then imagine how much water is being wasted. Take a few minutes to ensure these items are in good repair. A plumber may cost a few hundred dollars but will more than pay for himself in future savings!

Taking a few minutes a day can save thousands in a year...... Do you really think that you can not take the time to perform an energy checklist. It has been found that just using an energy checklist will save more that 10% of your utility bill. Take a minute and calculate how much you spent last year on utilities. If you just use a checklist and save 10% how much is that? Now let's suppose we do the audit, the checklist, a programmable thermostat, fans, and an equipment maintenance program..... 20%, 25%, more....... It is your money; why give it away!

NOTES

NOTES

INSURANCE COMPANY

Insurance is something you hope to never have to use. An item that you must have but with some luck never need to use the benefit of having. I will not spend a great deal of time on this topic but I do want to stress a few items. First off always have a good knowledge of your coverage. This does not mean become an agent; it means have the agent explain all coverage and why. Listen to recommendations from the agent but the last decision is yours. Talk to several agencies and get them to bid on your business. Ask questions that need answering:

1. What coverage; who will give you the best coverage for your business?

2. What cost for the coverage?

3. How well is the agency rated...... You may get a good deal only to find out the company does terrible with handling claims.

4. How long has the agency been around? Will they be around in 5, 10, or 20 years?

5. Do you like the agent? Are they responsive and understanding to your needs?

 **Shop a few before deciding what to do. Compare notes on recommended coverage's. Ask any and all questions that come to mind. If you feel they are not answering imagine what will happen when you really NEED them! Don't go with the cheapest unless they provide the best coverage, rating, and answer all the questions. When you do reach a decision and you return to lock in the policy discuss pricing. They may be able to find a reduction if you allow them the chance to get your business if they know that you are informed and have other quotes.**

MISC: ALARMS, TRASH, EXTERMINATOR, LINENS/TOWELS/ APRONS, MUSIC, ETC....

All the topics in this section may not apply to you now or ever. Maybe you have no alarm or even towel service. On the other hand you may be looking for one now and this with help give you guidance.

The key to saving money is being educated prior to spending the money!!!!!

Alarms

In today's world it is sad to say but most all businesses need alarms. Protecting your hard earned assets has become a high tech world. The criminals have become more and more educated therefore requiring alarm companies to improve technology. With this improvement comes added costs. The added costs are then introduced into added customer billing. On the other hand the competition has also increased in this field which help to maintain balance. It is critical to shop companies. The rates can swing as much as 50% from one company to another. Basic coverage will remain similar; the add on items are where the price really is driven up.

If when visiting a security company they use scare tactics to try and upsell additional camera or features walk away. You decide what you want up front and ask for a price structure. If they fail to provide.... WALK!

There are several factors to know before visiting these companies:

1. Does your location have a crime problem? Visit a local police department and ask.

2. Do you need outside security? After dark? Parking lot? Drive through?

3. Do you want to have cameras to cover key areas, safe, cash registers, back hallways?

4. Do you want to tape and if so do you have a secure location for a recorder?

5. Do you presently own your alarm system or do you need to buy one?

These are a few and your specific needs will generate more. Beware of add on items.

Last thought will be on contracts with the security companies. They will all want you to sign a three or more year contract. DON'T!!!!!!!!!!! They work for you. Let them know you will do a one year contract, you agree to review at the end of one year. A few will try the hard sell with equipment costs and try and get you to put a large up front payment out. Do not fall for this. You will find a company who wants your business who will offer a fair price, provide the equipment within the price, monitor you location, and give you a one year deal. Let them know that you will renew if their service is to the standard you need. At that point tell them that you want a 30 day out if you are not satisfied with their service. Do not let them tell you it does not need to be in the contract. Many companies say this then try to stiff you with a large penalty when you cancel them. Always make sure it is in writing in the contract signed by the alarm representative and yourself.

Trash

There are so many variables here I will not be able to cover them all. I will tell you what to look for and what to ask for when meeting with the local trash company. The best situation to find will be when you are in a city large enough to have more than one trash service. When you are in a situation where there is only one the options become much more limited.

Let's cover issues with a the small town with only one service first. Keep in mind some of these items will also be used in larger towns so please take the time to read both sections. The choices to bid against each other are obviously eliminated. The service cost may or may not be negotiated for base pick up. What I will cover is definitely in your corner to help you get the best cost for the service you need. You will need to know if at the present you are under any contract. If you are then get a copy and review. Look for the opportunity to review service. Request a meeting with your local representative. You may need to go to the local government building for the meeting depending on your town.

Questions to review:

1. Start with base price. Is there any better price plan available?

2. Review the frequency of pick up. This is the amount charged for each pick up per week. Do you have once, twice, more? Could you offer the Trash Company the ability to pick up less often? You save them money by saving them time.

3. Size of your receptacle. Could you get a larger dumpster and take less pickups? Most companies have several choices in dumpster size and if you went up one size then reduce the pick up frequency this will generally save money.

4. Recycle container. In the old day we were paid to recycle. Today you will have to pay them to do the pick up but at a significantly reduced price. If you have the space to have a second dumpster for paper the trash company will generally give you the second dumpster at less than half the regular dumpster price. Two things will happen with this: first you have the ability to put all you paper products into a different container thereby reducing the trash and reducing pickups. Second you have a large portion of your trash being picked up at half or less price!!! Of course this also helps the trash company and our environment at the same time.

For larger cities with trash service competition you can add this item to the above list:

The biggest difference is you can let the companies bid against each other. Get a list of the exact needs you have. Number of pick ups, size of dumpster, recycle or not, and give each a call. After you have a number from each then set up a meeting with each. Try and get them to beat each other! Rather fun to be honest!!!!

For both groups you never want to sign a long term agreement. When you have the opportunity to bid out the job every year companies are much less likely to try and jack up their prices each year. When you sign a three year or longer agreement there will be a clause that states there can be a rate increase proportionate to the increase the dump (place the trash company unloads) has every year. As dumps get filled the increase climb. On any given year that increase could be 50% or more! You need to agree to one year when at all possible!! If this is not possible then you need to cover the added years very detailed. You want them to agree to no more than a 10% hike each year as a maximum. You also want them to agree to a 30 day out if the service fails to meet expectation.

The last item is dumpster servicing. You want a new dumpster a minimum of twice a year. The truck is never allowed to compact on your parking lot. Then request that the dumpster area be cleaned once a year by the trash company. Reputable companies will agree to all these items!

Not only did you save money you cleaned up you image at the same time!

Exterminator

As with everything exterminators need to be bid against each other. There is one huge difference...... Whoever you end up with must take care of the bugs! The quickest way for a restaurant to go out of business is to have a bug or rodent problem. When you start shopping then have them supply references of business they service. Go and visit. Call the owners and discuss their satisfaction.

Issues to decide are:

1. Frequency of service.

2. Type of chemicals used. Any odor? Food safe?

3. Cleaning needed prior and after a service.

4. Call back for any problem before, during, or after hours.

5. Guarantee. If for any reason you are unhappy with the service all follow up calls are at no additional cost.

Of course they will also want a long term agreement. You don't. Make them give you a one year deal with the 30 day out and the understanding you will renew if they meet you expectation!!!

Linen Service

Bid Bid Bid Bid Bid Bid....... I think you get the point. This is a very flexible priced service. If you use towels, aprons, rugs, or napkins these all are vastly different cost with each company. Frequency of delivery, number needed, and how many items used are all huge in figuring the cost. Say you need 1,000 napkins, 100 aprons, and 5 rugs every 3 days. This will give you much greater bargaining power than if you only need 25 aprons and 2 rugs once a week. In the first position you are in control by offering a high volume drop on a regular basis. You are able to demand a better time for delivery. A better cost for having their service. A newer product delivered since you are a high volume customer.

On the other hand the small business has some ability to bargain but much less unfortunately. First get up a needs list and call around for bids. Once you have a few in hand then request a meeting with a couple. Get them to bid against each other and come to a final price. Once you do then you have a couple final decisions. Do you really need the service and at that price. Go to a local bulk laundry. Ask them what they charge for bulk items like towels and aprons to be cleaned and folded. Many such places charge only a few dollars per pound. Then go to a local restaurant supply and price bar towels and aprons. You may find it much cheaper to buy the items and have them cleaned. As your business grows you can always change your mind and go to the service but for now save the money!!!!!

Music

Not to beat a dead horse but the bid is the factor here also. Call around and get several people to come to your place and give you a bid. You probably don't need the high cost system but some background music. Low cost, few speakers, and not the 100 channel digital cable system. Forget the bells and whistles! Focus on your product and provide a nice soft background that in turn saves you money!!!!!!!!!!!!!!!!

Remember only one year and the equipment should be provided at a nominal cost!!!!!

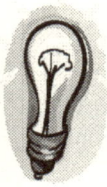

The customer will be much happier if the money you save is used to improve your product!!!!!!!

NOTES

NOTES

EXAMPLES OF COST SAVINGS TO PROFIT

- BASE PROFIT & LOSS STATEMENT

- COST OF GOODS SAVINGS

- LABOR SAVINGS

- UTILITY SAVINGS

- MISCELLANIOUS SAVINGS

- COMPLETE SAVINGS REVIEW

FORM REVIEW PAGE

EXAMPLE PROFIT AND LOSS STATEMENT				
LINE ITEM	**DOLLARS/ MONTH**	**PERCENT**	**DOLLARS/YEAR**	**NOTES**
SALES	$100,000.00		$1,200,000.00	
TAX	($825.00)		($9,900.00)	
NET	$99,175.00		$1,190,100.00	
COST OF GOODS	($37,000.00)	37%	($444,000.00)	
PAPER COST	($9,000.00)	9%	($108,000.00)	
SUPPLIES/JANITORIAL	($3,000.00)	3%	($36,000.00)	
TOTAL	($49,000.00)	49%	($588,000.00)	
NET	$50,175.00		$602,100.00	
SALARY	($7,000.00)	7%	($84,000.00)	
HOURLY	($30,000.00)	30%	($360,000.00)	
TOTAL	($37,000.00)	37%	($444,000.00)	
NET	$13,175.00		$158,100.00	
RENT	($9,000.00)	9%	($108,000.00)	
UTILITIES / GAS	($500.00)	0.50%	($6,000.00)	
UTILITIES / ELEC	($3,000.00)	3%	($36,000.00)	
UTILITIES / WATER	($500.00)	0.50%	($6,000.00)	
TOTAL	($13,000.00)		($156,000.00)	
NET	$175.00		$2,100.00	
MISC:				
REPAIR AND MAINTENANCE	($500.00)	0.50%	($6,000.00)	
OFFICE SUPPLIES	($300.00)	0.30%	($3,600.00)	
ADVERTISING	($4,000.00)	4%	($48,000.00)	
EQUIPMENT	($1,000.00)	1%	($12,000.00)	
CASH OVER/SHORT	($200.00)	0.20%	($2,400.00)	
ALARM	($300.00)	0.30%	($3,600.00)	
MUSIC	($100.00)	0.10%	($1,200.00)	
TRASH	($400.00)	0.40%	($4,800.00)	
OTHER	($200.00)	0.20%	($2,400.00)	
TOTAL	($7,000.00)		($84,000.00)	
NET	($6,825.00)		($81,900.00)	
THE BOTTOM LINE	($6,825.00)		($81,900.00)	

EXAMPLE PROFIT AND LOSS STATEMENT
SHOWING 26% REDUCTION IN COST OF GOODS

LINE ITEM	DOLLARS/ MONTH	PERCENT	DOLLARS/YEAR	NOTES
SALES	$100,000.00		$1,200,000.00	
TAX	($825.00)		($9,900.00)	
NET	$99,175.00		$1,190,100.00	
COST OF GOODS	($30,000.00)	30%	($360,000.00)	
PAPER COST	($4,000.00)	4%	($48,000.00)	
SUPPLIES/JANITORIAL	($2,000.00)	2%	($24,000.00)	
TOTAL	($36,000.00)	36%	($432,000.00)	
NET	$63,175.00		$758,100.00	
SALARY	($7,000.00)	7%	($84,000.00)	
HOURLY	($30,000.00)	30%	($360,000.00)	
TOTAL	($37,000.00)	37%	($444,000.00)	
NET	$26,175.00		$314,100.00	
RENT	($9,000.00)	9%	($108,000.00)	
UTILITIES / GAS	($500.00)	0.50%	($6,000.00)	
UTILITIES / ELEC	($3,000.00)	3%	($36,000.00)	
UTILITIES / WATER	($500.00)	0.50%	($6,000.00)	
TOTAL	($13,000.00)		($156,000.00)	
NET	$13,175.00		$158,100.00	
MISC:				
REPAIR AND MAINTENANCE	($500.00)	0.50%	($6,000.00)	
OFFICE SUPPLIES	($300.00)	0.30%	($3,600.00)	
ADVERTISING	($4,000.00)	4%	($48,000.00)	
EQUIPMENT	($1,000.00)	1%	($12,000.00)	
CASH OVER/SHORT	($200.00)	0.20%	($2,400.00)	
ALARM	($300.00)	0.30%	($3,600.00)	
MUSIC	($100.00)	0.10%	($1,200.00)	
TRASH	($400.00)	0.40%	($4,800.00)	
OTHER	($200.00)	0.20%	($2,400.00)	
TOTAL	($7,000.00)		($84,000.00)	
NET	$6,175.00		$74,100.00	
THE BOTTOM LINE	$6,175.00		$74,100.00	

140

EXAMPLE PROFIT AND LOSS STATEMENT
SHOWING 15% REDUCTION IN LABOR USING FORMAT FROM BOOK

LINE ITEM	DOLLARS/MONTH	PERCENT	DOLLARS/YEAR	NOTES
SALES	$100,000.00		$1,200,000.00	
TAX	($825.00)		($9,900.00)	
NET	$99,175.00		$1,190,100.00	
COST OF GOODS	($37,000.00)	37%	($444,000.00)	
PAPER COST	($9,000.00)	9%	($108,000.00)	
SUPPLIES/JANITORIAL	($3,000.00)	3%	($36,000.00)	
TOTAL	($49,000.00)	49%	($588,000.00)	
NET	$50,175.00		$602,100.00	
SALARY	($7,000.00)	7%	($84,000.00)	
HOURLY	($25,000.00)	25%	($300,000.00)	
TOTAL	($32,000.00)	32%	($384,000.00)	
NET	$18,175.00		$218,100.00	
RENT	($9,000.00)	9%	($108,000.00)	
UTILITIES / GAS	($500.00)	0.50%	($6,000.00)	
UTILITIES / ELEC	($3,000.00)	3%	($36,000.00)	
UTILITIES / WATER	($500.00)	0.50%	($6,000.00)	
TOTAL	($13,000.00)		($156,000.00)	
NET	$5,175.00		$62,100.00	
MISC:				
REPAIR AND MAINTENANCE	($500.00)	0.50%	($6,000.00)	
OFFICE SUPPLIES	($300.00)	0.30%	($3,600.00)	
ADVERTISING	($4,000.00)	4%	($48,000.00)	
EQUIPMENT	($1,000.00)	1%	($12,000.00)	
CASH OVER/SHORT	($200.00)	0.20%	($2,400.00)	
ALARM	($300.00)	0.30%	($3,600.00)	
MUSIC	($100.00)	0.10%	($1,200.00)	
TRASH	($400.00)	0.40%	($4,800.00)	
OTHER	($200.00)	0.20%	($2,400.00)	
TOTAL	($7,000.00)		($84,000.00)	
NET	($1,825.00)		($21,900.00)	
THE BOTTOM LINE	($1,825.00)		($21,900.00)	

G. Cole Harned

EXAMPLE PROFIT AND LOSS STATEMENT
SHOWING 12.5% UTILITY SAVINGS

LINE ITEM	DOLLARS/ MONTH	PERCENT	DOLLARS/YEAR	NOTES
SALES	$100,000.00		$1,200,000.00	
TAX	($825.00)		($9,900.00)	
NET	$99,175.00		$1,190,100.00	
COST OF GOODS	($37,000.00)	37%	($444,000.00)	
PAPER COST	($9,000.00)	9%	($108,000.00)	
SUPPLIES/JANITORIAL	($3,000.00)	3%	($36,000.00)	
TOTAL	($49,000.00)	49%	($588,000.00)	
NET	$50,175.00		$602,100.00	
SALARY	($7,000.00)	7%	($84,000.00)	
HOURLY	($30,000.00)	30%	($360,000.00)	
TOTAL	($37,000.00)	37%	($444,000.00)	
NET	$13,175.00		$158,100.00	
RENT	($9,000.00)	9%	($108,000.00)	
UTILITIES / GAS	($400.00)	0.40%	($4,800.00)	
UTILITIES / ELEC	($2,700.00)	0.27%	($32,400.00)	
UTILITIES / WATER	($400.00)	0.40%	($4,800.00)	
TOTAL	($12,500.00)		($150,000.00)	
NET	$675.00		$8,100.00	
MISC:				
REPAIR AND MAINTENANCE	($500.00)	0.50%	($6,000.00)	
OFFICE SUPPLIES	($300.00)	0.30%	($3,600.00)	
ADVERTISING	($4,000.00)	4%	($48,000.00)	
EQUIPMENT	($1,000.00)	1%	($12,000.00)	
CASH OVER/SHORT	($200.00)	0.20%	($2,400.00)	
ALARM	($300.00)	0.30%	($3,600.00)	
MUSIC	($100.00)	0.10%	($1,200.00)	
TRASH	($400.00)	0.40%	($4,800.00)	
OTHER	($200.00)	0.20%	($2,400.00)	
TOTAL	($7,000.00)		($84,000.00)	
NET	($6,325.00)		($75,900.00)	
THE BOTTOM LINE	($6,325.00)		($75,900.00)	

EXAMPLE PROFIT AND LOSS STATEMENT
SHOWING 1.6% REDUCTION IN MISCELLANEOUS

LINE ITEM	DOLLARS/ MONTH	PERCENT	DOLLARS/YEAR	NOTES
SALES	$100,000.00		$1,200,000.00	
TAX	($825.00)		($9,900.00)	
NET	$99,175.00		$1,190,100.00	
COST OF GOODS	($37,000.00)	37%	($444,000.00)	
PAPER COST	($9,000.00)	9%	($108,000.00)	
SUPPLIES/JANITORIAL	($3,000.00)	3%	($36,000.00)	
TOTAL	($49,000.00)	49%	($586,000.00)	
NET	$50,175.00		$602,100.00	
SALARY	($7,000.00)	7%	($84,000.00)	
HOURLY	($30,000.00)	30%	($360,000.00)	
TOTAL	($37,000.00)	37%	($444,000.00)	
NET	$13,175.00		$158,100.00	
RENT	($9,000.00)	9%	($108,000.00)	
UTILITIES / GAS	($500.00)	0.50%	($6,000.00)	
UTILITIES / ELEC	($3,000.00)	3%	($36,000.00)	
UTILITIES / WATER	($500.00)	0.50%	($6,000.00)	
TOTAL	($13,000.00)		($156,000.00)	
NET	$175.00		$2,100.00	
MISC:				
REPAIR AND MAINTENANCE	($500.00)	0.50%	($6,000.00)	
OFFICE SUPPLIES	($200.00)	0.20%	($2,400.00)	
ADVERTISING	($4,000.00)	4%	($48,000.00)	
EQUIPMENT	($500.00)	0.50%	($6,000.00)	
CASH OVER/SHORT	($200.00)	0.20%	($2,400.00)	
ALARM	($50.00)	0.05%	($600.00)	
MUSIC	($50.00)	0.05%	($600.00)	
TRASH	($150.00)	0.15%	($1,800.00)	
OTHER	($200.00)	0.20%	($2,400.00)	
TOTAL	($5,850.00)		($70,200.00)	
NET	($5,675.00)		($68,100.00)	
THE BOTTOM LINE	($5,675.00)		($68,100.00)	

EXAMPLE PROFIT AND LOSS STATEMENT				
TOTAL PROJECTED SAVINGS FROM BOOK USAGE				
LINE ITEM	DOLLARS/ MONTH	PERCENT	DOLLARS/YEAR	NOTES
SALES	$100,000.00		$1,200,000.00	
TAX	($825.00)		($9,900.00)	
NET	$99,175.00		$1,190,100.00	
COST OF GOODS	($30,000.00)	30%	($360,000.00)	
PAPER COST	($4,000.00)	4%	($48,000.00)	
SUPPLIES/JANITORIAL	($2,000.00)	2%	($24,000.00)	
TOTAL	($36,000.00)	36%	($432,000.00)	
NET	$63,175.00		$758,100.00	
SALARY	($7,000.00)	7%	($84,000.00)	
HOURLY	($25,000.00)	25%	($300,000.00)	
TOTAL	($32,000.00)	32%	($384,000.00)	
NET	$31,175.00		$374,100.00	
RENT	($9,000.00)	9%	($108,000.00)	
UTILITIES / GAS	($400.00)	0.40%	($4,800.00)	
UTILITIES / ELEC	($2,700.00)	0.27%	($32,400.00)	
UTILITIES / WATER	($400.00)	0.40%	($4,800.00)	
TOTAL	($12,500.00)		($150,000.00)	
NET	$18,675.00		$224,100.00	
MISC:				
REPAIR AND MAINTENANCE	($500.00)	0.50%	($6,000.00)	
OFFICE SUPPLIES	($200.00)	0.20%	($2,400.00)	
ADVERTISING	($4,000.00)	4%	($48,000.00)	
EQUIPMENT	($500.00)	0.50%	($6,000.00)	
CASH OVER/SHORT	($200.00)	0.20%	($2,400.00)	
ALARM	($50.00)	0.05%	($600.00)	
MUSIC	($50.00)	0.05%	($600.00)	
TRASH	($150.00)	0.15%	($1,800.00)	
OTHER	($200.00)	0.20%	($2,400.00)	
TOTAL	($5,850.00)		($70,200.00)	
NET	$12,825.00		$153,900.00	
THE BOTTOM LINE	$12,825.00		$153,900.00	

CONCLUSION

CONGRATULATIONS!!!!

You have just completed a thorough workbook to help guide you to a better and brighter future in business. Whether you bought this book to run your own business more profitably or you work for a company and wanted to get pointers to help you earn a promotion; you have in your hands a wealth of information. It took me a lifetime to compile this information and put it down in an easy to understand handbook. A handbook for everyone; not just the business executive but the small business owner who wants the same chance to succeed as the big businesses.

No matter the reason for your choice of reading this book you have made that choice to improve your chance of a better future in business. I have heard many times that the small business can not make it in today's economy......... That chance for you has just improved. By reading this book you will have a hand up on most of your competition. Even many of the big businesses will be amazed at your success. They will wonder how you can charge less while providing a better product. They will marvel at your ability to hire and maintain the brightest employees. Will be in astonishment as they watch you thrive while they struggle to maintain.

The name of my company is called Choices or Chances. This is because life is all about the choices we make and the chances we take. This book will help you to reduce your _chance_ of failure and by buying it you have made the _choice_ to have a better run business. You have made the _choice_ to improve and take less _chance_.

I will not kid you about the food business. It is a tough world. When you follow these guidelines you will give yourself better than a fighting chance to make it. I truly believe that anyone who follows the advice I have laid out in this book **WILL** succeed.

You will improve your BOTTOM LINE.......

And that my friends is.........

The Bottom Line

www.ingramcontent.com/pod-product-compliance
Lightning Source LLC
Chambersburg PA
CBHW032024170526
45157CB00002B/843